la luce vince sempre

the light always wins

sophia marie

to tricia
thank you for helping me to
see the light

foreword

this book was born from journal entries written in the notes app on my phone while i was in the midst of the darkest period of my life. i struggled with anxiety, depression, a severe eating disorder, sexual assault, and self harm (amongst other things). the entries have been edited to avoid being too graphic, but they are raw nonetheless (and still might be triggering).

writing these words was my way of coping with intense emotions and very dark thoughts. but even though many of these poems contain immense pain, they also reveal a journey of growth. not the clean, linear kind, but the kind of growth that happens slowly, has setbacks, and hurts, but happens nonetheless.

sharing these vulnerable words is scary, but i believe there is a lot of power in doing so. my hope is that they can help someone to feel a little less alone in their own journey. to feel heard and understood. and even if you don't relate to these poems, i hope that you can see that it is possible to overcome whatever challenge or darkness life throws at you.

because i was once a girl who could see nothing but darkness and wasn't sure she'd ever emerge from that.
but, with the help of a lot of people, slowly but surely i did, and i began to have faith that there would be light on the other side.

living in that light is worth every tear and ounce of pain to find. and i believe you can find it, too. because the light always wins.

table of contents

chapter 1: numb...1

chapter 2: breaking...............................13

chapter 3: climbing..............................23

chapter 4: holding on........................33

chapter 5: pondering.........................45

chapter 6: feeling...............................59

chapter 7: growing.............................71

chapter 1
numb

lost

i'm lost
wandering around aimlessly
not sure what to do or where to go

i thought i'd find happiness by being small
my life's purpose was to achieve that goal

but now i'm left stranded
every scrap of direction is out the window
so i wander aimlessly
searching for a purpose
wishing for a guide
any way out of this hell i've dug myself into
perhaps a hell i deserve to be in

but what i do know is that i can't stay here
i know it will be the end of me if i do
so i will continue to wander
to search for a way out
a way to be anywhere but here

tired

my body feels like lead
each step feels like a job
like i'm walking through quicksand

thoughts run rampant through my head
an untamable whirlwind of anxiety and self-depreciation
and an overbearing aura of darkness

every day i am being pulled apart
"get better."
but you don't deserve to
"recover"
but you aren't sick enough

each day feels a little harder
and my reservoirs of willpower are running dry
i'm running on fumes
and i don't know how many more days i can buy

numb

nothing
i feel nothing at all
there is a pit in my chest where i'm supposed to feel
but it is empty

i float through life
doing what i need to
but it's just a practiced dance
a routine rehearsed to a t
there is no thought, no energy, no emotion

everything seems dull and flavorless
i question the meaning of anything

but at least this way i can survive
at least this way i am not in pain

the machine

i think i was only built to achieve
my life is clockwork
an assembly line
a symphony of responsibilities and desires colliding
moving from one task to the next

my only goal is to do as much as i can
with the time i am given
i need no rest
i have no room for emotion
my task is to
go go *go*
produce produce *produce*
succeed succeed *succeed*

never fail, never waiver
and if i fall short, not only have i failed
but i am a failure

the game is rigged
no matter what i do, i fall short
because how can i know if what i did
was everything i *could* do?
and if i didn't do my task to the max
if i didn't use every ounce of myself
then i haven't truly succeeded

an endless journey

days wear on
in and out
meal after meal
wearing me down
chipping my soul away

every time i make progress, i just realize how far i have to go
it feels like climbing a mountain
only each time i reach the peak, another appears in front of me
and my only option is to climb
or fall to my death

so i climb
even when my grip becomes weak
and it feels much easier to just let go
i keep going in hopes that
one day
i'll reach the true summit

push and pull

i've set myself on this journey
i chose recovery
but little did i know that it would be much, much more
than that singular decision

each day i am tugged and pulled
the temptation of returning to poisonous behaviors
to restriction, weighing myself, exercising
a siren sings it's sweet serenade
promising that if i come back, it will make me happy

but i made a commitment
and i know it's what i need to do
even if my heart isn't fully there
even if more of me wants to quit than keep going

because i know the siren is lying
so i plug my ears
and resist the tug that is pulling me
stand my ground the best i can
and keep moving forward on this path

the beast

there is a beast in my mind
i try my best to keep it at bay

i hired guards to keep it contained
but they are not perfect
they rely on the presence of others
when i party, they do too
and when i am alone and the guards are down
the beast comes out to play

when the beast breaks free, it consumes me
it rampages through my mind
and holds every other part of me prisoner
it reminds me of everything i'm not, but should be
it reprimands me for everything i am, but shouldn't be
it tells me i am a failure
that i am a burden
that i am worthless
that i have no purpose
that i should just give up

the beast knows the pain i am in
it tells me i deserve every ounce of it
but it also tells me how to make it go away
but the cost is destroying myself

the beast wants me in pain
because when i am in pain, i'm willing to listen and act
and destroy myself
so the beast doesn't have to

i am the beast

when you realize

that you're just hanging on
waiting
for when you can live
instead of just existing
or just getting by
just getting through whatever your current task is

until you realize
that you've never given yourself the chance or permission to just *live*
to enjoy the present moment
to notice and appreciate the little things
to show yourself love
to be loved and not question why
or feel like you don't deserve it

you've never allowed yourself to believe
that you have a purpose
that your life is worth living
that you will fulfill the potential everyone says you have
that all the possibilities of joy are worth the suffering it will take to get
there
that you are worth something beyond your appearance and size
or how productive you are
or what you achieve

that the simple act of trying, even when you don't want to
or think you can
or think it's not going to be worth it
is enough

that you will *ever* be enough
that you will *ever* be worthy of the love that's poured into you
that you are allowed to live for yourself instead of staying
just so you don't hurt those who love you

when you realize all this, it's enough to break you
because you don't know if you'll ever get to a place where you do accept
these things
and find a life that is truly worth living

holding on

i keep telling myself to hold on until...
until something
i'm not sure what

i'm waiting for someone or something to save me
but no person or thing can save me from myself
the only person who can truly do that is me
and i don't think i can

dark thoughts weigh me down
they burden my existence

i'm scared
i'm scared that i am going to lose hope
and i am beginning to think this is all pointless

so i grasp onto a single strand of hope
grip it so tightly that it burns
melding into my flesh
so that even when i don't think i can hold on any longer
even when my grip loosens and i'm hanging on by a thread
i will continue holding on
and waiting
waiting for it to be worth it

drowning

i sit by the sea
watching as the tide ebbs and flows
waves swell and crash to the shore
white caps frothing and foaming near my feet

i can't help but notice the enormity and power of the ocean
it makes me feel as small as my mind makes me feel

thoughts crash over me just like the waves
wishing those powerful torrents would sweep me away
wishing they could somehow strip away the pain
thinking it'd be better if i wasn't here
that i have no purpose

they crash over me
swallow me whole
and i am defenseless against their cold, brutal words
leaving me drowning, gasping for air
kicking, screaming, thrashing

i want to submit
want to feel the release of letting go
of stopping the fight

but i can't
and i have never been a quitter before
so i damn well will try

chapter 2
breaking

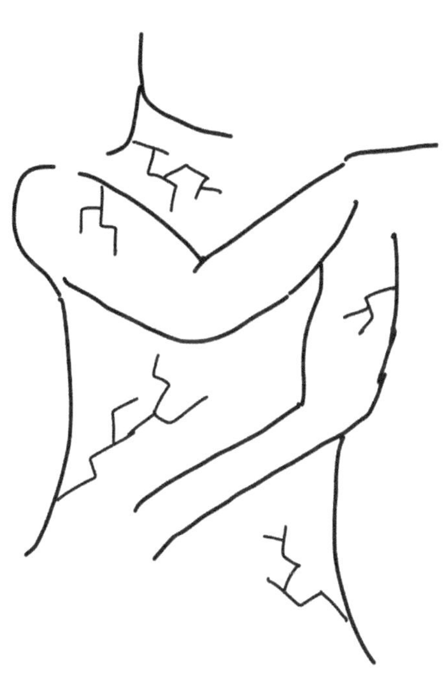

betrayal

he made me feel wanted
he convinced me i was worth something
that i could be something to someone

the first night was heaven
i'd never been touched that way before
been looked at that way before
felt *wanted* like that before

so i trusted him
because i was desperate
and i was scared that he might be the only one who could possibly want
me

i gave myself to him
fell asleep in his arms
but then he took everything from me

he used me like a tool
made me feel worthless
treated me like his property
then threw me away like garbage

all that was left was a broken girl
crumbled on the floor
with an endless stream of tears streaming down her face
a pit inside where something else once filled
a looming sense that she will never be wanted again
and trust that might be broken
forevermore

spiraling

i'm spiraling spiraling spiraling
spinning out of control
a chaotic jumble of emotion and pain
a top falling apart as it rotates
i am unable to save me from myself

i thought i'd hit rock bottom by now
but it turns out i can go deeper than i imagined
burrowing into the ground
suffocating by my own doing

what if i get so deep
that i never see the light again?

running

i'm running from myself
but there's nowhere to hide
i'm afraid she's going to catch me
and destroy me from within

i've become an expert at evading
i work and study and exercise and party
and go, go, go
so i don't have time to think
to feel
to let her catch up to me

but sometimes she does
and she is ruthless
she preys on my deepest insecurities
she tears into my soul
worthless
failure
never enough

she makes me feel small
she makes me want to disappear
she makes me want to quit altogether
because clearly there is not point in trying
she is impossible to appease

i can't escape her because she is stronger than i am
i have no choice but to submit
she holds my mind prisoner
she owns my life
because even when she hasn't caught me
i am always running

mirrorball

i am a mirrorball
always wanting to be noticed
but never seeking attention

i fade into the background
i blend in with any crowd
i'm afraid to stand out
but wish anyone would reach out to me

i've always tried so hard to fit in
to feel like i belong
but it always feels forced
and i never feel like i'm actually wanted
instead i feel invisible
but somehow only at times when i don't want to be

i'm fragile, but on the outside i seem strong
i'm broken, but i appear put together
i mask and hide and blend in
i smile when i'm in pain
i laugh when i feel hollow
afraid to show the truth
afraid to appear too different

it's an innate part of me
i will always be a mirrorball

softness

i have never wanted to be soft
or at least, i was afraid to be

i hate my body because it is soft
i thought being mentally soft would lead me to fail
i feared being emotionally soft because i didn't want to get hurt

so i tore down my body until it was hard
and i lived with discipline and force
and built my walls high so they could not be penetrated

but what if softness isn't all that bad?

a softer body makes for better hugs
a softer mind gives room for rest and slowness so the little joys of life
can be savored
and tearing down those walls allows love to be given and received and
true emotion to be felt
the things that make me human
the things that might make me feel whole again

because i want to enjoy the soft things in life
and i want to receive love that is soft and tender and intimate
i want to *love* and *feel* and *live*
and i can't do that without softness

lost cause

i can't help but feel
that i am a lost cause
not worth saving
not worth the energy
not worth the care

because no one can save me from myself
from the beast that lies within
and why should they anyway?
what do i provide?
what do i give to anyone?

i wish
this pain
would go away
and i didn't have to be saved

love & life

"i'd die for you"
they say it's the greatest expression of love
to sacrifice everything you have for another
but i think that's wrong

instead, i say
"i'll live for you"
because i can't take away something they love
and bring them pain
and tear them apart

it's still a sacrifice
and it still hurts
but it is worth it
to stay for those you love

consent

there should be a consent form to love me
because no one should have to deal with all of this unknowingly

the broken
the ugly
the hurt
the needy
always looking for someone to see what she cannot
always feeling like she can never be worthy of love

i don't think anyone would love me if they knew all of me
i am too much to take on
i am not good enough to deserve that love
and all the sacrifice that comes with it

so i come with a disclaimer:
damaged
caution
handle with care
be prepared
because i am much more than i appear on the surface
and i am a lot to carry

chapter 3
climbing

forgiveness

i took a journey through time
read old journal entries from a time past
a time when i was consumed by a demon in my head
that demon was starving me

i had convinced myself that it was my fault
that i chose to do it to myself
and i hated myself for that

but reading it now, outside of that head
it's suddenly so clear
i see a girl who was struggling and didn't know why
a girl so unaware of the forces at play
who had much less control than she thought

and i've realized that it wasn't true
it was there before
i didn't chose it
it wasn't my fault

this realization hit me like a wrecking ball
crashing right through my chest
and it hurt
and i cried and shook and *felt* it

and then, a release
a weight off my chest
because i forgave myself
i showed myself compassion
something that i once thought was impossible

i think this is what healing feels like

validation

i am a master gaslighter
i will convince myself i am fine when i'm not
and i will minimize any struggle i have
if i feel okay one day, then every other bad one didn't count
so i dig myself deeper
never thinking i'm "bad enough" or "sick enough"
to deserve help

i yearned to be understood
for my problems to have a label, a stamp of validity
for someone to see me and know that what i'm going through is real
that it is difficult to handle
that i deserve help

but now i know
even without a name
even when it's not visible
even when it's not as severe as others'
my struggles are real
and it's okay to struggle with them
and not only do they warrant receiving help,
but it takes a lot of vulnerability and strength to seek it

to anyone who relates to this:
i see you
i feel you
please know that your struggles are valid, too
and you deserve all the support and care to help you overcome them

fighter

i signed up for this
i decided to give recovery another shot
and throw myself into bootcamp to learn to eat again

this is by far the hardest thing i have ever done
each meal in program is a new battle
more intense than i could have ever imagined
the thoughts come at me like a barrage of punches
and i have to stand there and take it
being beaten to a pulp like rocky balboa

but each bite i take is a blow to my opponent
and i always survive another round
with sheer willpower and commitment to trying this
i somehow haven't been knocked out

in fact, in many ways
i keep winning
because simply staying is winning
remaining standing is winning
completing a meal is winning
even when i feel like i had to give everything for it
even though it's the last thing i want to do
even though i am oh so tired of fighting

i persevere
i fight for a chance at a better life
one that i hardly think i deserve
just in case i do
just in case it's worth it
because, at heart
i am a fighter

letting go

it's time
it's time to let go
to let go of restriction and control
i don't have a choice
it's the only way out

this body is what made me feel wanted and accepted
or maybe *worthy* of being wanted and accepted
and it is tearing me apart to throw it away
because *god,*
i wanted it *so* fucking bad for *so* long
and i've been holding onto it with every ounce of strength
i beg and plead for it to stop growing
but i can't control that either

day after day after day
i have to do the thing that i *know* will destroy my most prized possession
so when it feels impossible
when it tears me apart
i tell myself to do this, just for today
just for this meal
just for this bite
prying open the steel grip with my own mind
slowly but surely letting go
in hopes that i'll be able to hold onto something better

banana bread

tonight i baked banana bread
and listened to taylor swift
and drank wine

it was a simple night, spent alone
but it wasn't so simple for me
because when i baked my banana bread,
i knew i'd have a slice
and i nibbled at the chocolate chips
and i licked the bowl
and i smiled
because not too long ago, i wouldn't dare do any of that
and if i did, i'd punish for myself for it
i'd feel guilty
and unworthy
of a simple pleasure

a pleasure i finally let myself have and cherish
a pleasure that maybe, just maybe, i deserve to have

making banana bread may seem simple
but to me, it means progress and growth and hope
hope for what life can be
hope for how it can be filled with little moments of joy and light
hope that all of this will be worth it

i believe it will be worth it

falling

i'm falling apart
ripping to shreds

every day i have to choose to do something that is hard and painful
and i don't know if i can keep going

i don't think i can live with myself like *that*
how could i when i can hardly stand myself like *this*?

trapped

i feel trapped in my own body
a body that is now foreign
a body that no longer feels like it's mine

i can't escape it
i am contained wherever i go
i pound on the walls but they won't budge
my hands search frantically for an exit that doesn't exist
my chest tightens
i feel claustrophobic as they press in on me

and to change it would be to give up everything i've been
fighting for and working for
it would be returning to a different, special kind of hell
a hell with no promise of escape

i'm told i won't always feel like this
that one day, the walls will release
and this body will feel like a home, not a prison
so until then i sit and wait
and try not to suffocate
praying that one day i will be able to breathe again
and i will no longer be trapped

strong

for a long time, i've refused to think i was strong
i thought that everything i did was the bare minimum
that i was just doing what i had to do
just getting by
and that is not strength, that's just not being a failure

i never thought i should be applauded
for doing basic human tasks
no. real strength was going above and beyond
succeeding despite have to endure the worst challenges

i thought all of my struggles were my fault
and even if they weren't, they weren't that bad
when it felt hard i thought i was being weak
overexaggerating
making excuses for when i did inevitably fail

but i am starting to realize that it isn't my fault
and even if others have struggles, that doesn't mean that mine aren't
difficult to handle, too

in fact, i'm starting to realize how hard what i'm doing is
and how much i've gone through
i'm starting to unearth and feel all the pain underneath
and it is a LOT
i have a feeling that not everyone would keep going
hell, i've almost given up many times
it would be a lot easier not to continue

but i do
i keep going
even when it's hard
even when i don't want to
even when it hurts
even when it feels impossible
even when it feels like i am physically breaking
even when my soul is shattering
i show up and i keep pushing day after day

if anyone else told me this, i'd think they're pretty damn strong
because not giving up is strong
surviving this is strong

so i'm starting to believe
that i am strong too

chapter 4
holding on

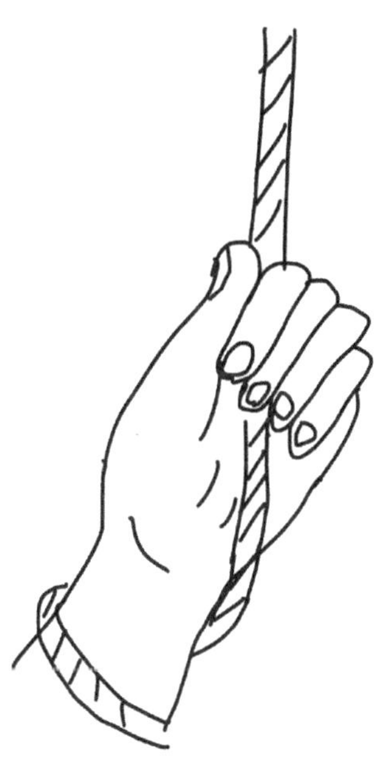

a rose

a rose has always been an important symbol to me
my friend's middle name
a religious symbol
a representation of my grandmother

but i am finding that i am a rose, too
i am also soft
i feel deeply
i love deeply
i thought i had to be tough, so i grew thorns
and i always feel bad that i need to be tended to
because i thought i should be able to bloom on my own

but no one would say a rose is any less beautiful because it is delicate
in fact, that's part of its beauty
they are so beautiful that it is worth all the care and work it takes to see
it and all of it's intricate, delicate beauty

so yes, i think i am a rose
and there's so much beauty in that

who am i?

i am beginning to find myself
the person that is me

more than a brain
more than a body
more than accolades
more than achievements

she is kind
she is curious
she feels deeply, loves deeply
she is loyal
she is funny

she is a sister, friend, daughter, cousin
and finally
she is starting to live

ripping, tearing, shredding

i can't be in this body anymore
i'm all too aware of it
every ounce is too much
my soul clenches and thrashed and turns

i need outoutout
i want to rip and tear and shred myself apart
like a wild beast with claws of steel
every bit of skin
of extra flesh
it must be gone

the desire is feral
i want to dispose of every inadequacy
to destroy every single part of me that i don't like
it shouldn't exist
i can't bear it's presence any longer
i would give anything
anything
to have a body better, *smaller* than the one i own

so i do tear my skin
the pain offers a momentary reprieve
but the flaws are still there
no matter how much i rip, tear, and shred
they always will be

low

i feel so low and i don't know why
surrounded by friends
doing things i love and have looked forward to
yet my mind is consumed by darkness

if i can't enjoy these things, what's the point?
i'm afraid my life is just going to be a game of waiting
for the next wave of darkness
that i will never escape this cycle

i hate that i can't control these thoughts
they come from me, so why can't i?
it makes me feel so helpless
and they are going deeper than ever

it's either live like this, in this body, and be miserable
or starve and be miserable
there is no way out
i can't stop the images entering my mind
my entire being wants to leave
but i know i can't
i would never forgive myself

i yearn for an escape
to feel anything but this
because everything feels impossible
i am tired of fighting
and i question what i've been fighting for in the first place

stay

stay
please stay

stay so you can give your siblings another hug
stay so you can smell fresh autumn air
stay so you can sing in the car
stay so you can bake
stay so you can go to class with your best friends

stay so you can fall in love
stay so you can see the world
stay so you can have a kid

stay until you can say you've lived
stay until you've loved with everything in you
until the infinite reservoir has run dry
find a reason
any reason
just please please stay

at least one more day
please stay

time and time again

time and time again
i feel like i've failed
i don't want to do what i know i need to do
i don't know if i *can* do what i need to do
meal after meal, day after day
i feel like i'm broken

but time and time again
i let it hurt
and then i get up
and dry my tears
and do it anyway

for the hope that one day
it'll be the last time i have to do that
and i will be whole again

stars

sometimes i gaze at the stars
and i wish i was in the sky with them
instead of being planted on the ground

sometimes i look up
and i see a million bright lights
i remember how small i am
it can make me feel insignificant
but sometimes it puts my worries into perspective

sometimes the stars give me hope
they remind me of all there is to see
and all that my life can be

sometimes the stars remind me of the ones i love but have lost
i wonder if they are up there, looking down at me
i wonder if they are proud of me
i wonder if they know how much i loved them
how much i still love them
how they are often my reason

but the best thing about stars
is that they shine oh so brightly
and they shine even when i can't see them
they are proof that there is always light
even if you can't see it right now

body

every time i go out
i am reminded of what i wish i was

and every time i look in the mirror
i am reminded of everything i will never be

and sometimes that realization
rips me to shreds
and makes me want to disappear

god, why do i have to look like this?
and why do i have to care about it?

poison sweet poison

i know it's bad for me
but my mind pulls me toward it anyway

it blunts the edge of pain
allows me to escape myself
even for just a bit
to pretend that i am cool and accepted
someone who is fun and lively and spontaneous

but somewhere along the line
i started sipping this sweet poison alone
a glass turned into a bottle
one night turned into three and four and five

it wasn't my own hand reaching to pour another
not my own feet walking toward the fridge
or walking to my car to buy another bottle for the night

i've convinced myself i can stop
that i just don't want to
but anytime i try
some excuse pops up
and i have poison in my system again

it is my vice, my captor, my protector, my keeper
it has convinced me i need it
that i will be nothing, enjoy nothing without it
and i can't seem to leave it

the mirror

a simple plane of glass
the truth-teller, the reality

at one time, the mirror confirmed my worth
because it showed a body smaller than its previous form
yet always provided a map for how to improve

it enamored me
trapped me in its gaze
time froze
and i spent eternity finding every inadequacy
every fault
every failure
until i snapped and wished there was nothing in the mirror at all

now i can barely gaze in any reflective surface
when i do, my heart drops
because it confirms my lack of worth
that i am, completely and wholly, inadequate
too big, too much, too flawed

but the mirror isn't the truth-teller
because my mind warps and bends its images
i cannot trust what i see

but still, it hurts me more than anything
i crumble and snap and break in it's grasp
because the mirror tells me that i will
never
ever
be enough

chapter 5
pondering

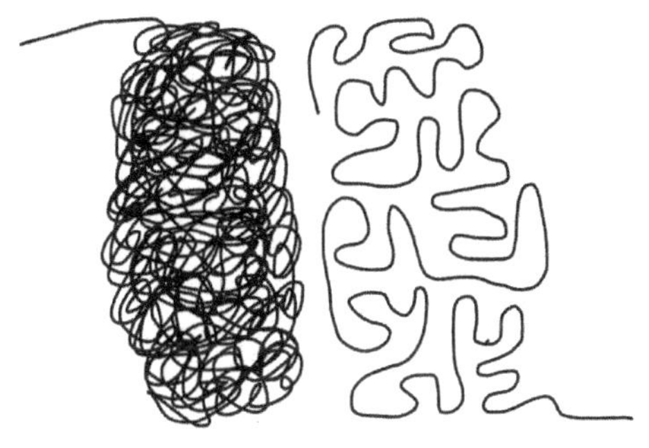

anna

i see you in the soft things in my life
the way the autumn leaves fall
and the way the sun rises
there's no coincidence it's the soft pink of a rose

it took me a long time to appreciate these things
to even remotely like myself
because i always have felt like i was never doing enough
honestly, i still feel that way a lot of days
it's really hard to see through the darkness

but i've been growing, and i am strong
just like you were strong

i still think about you so often
and i'm sorry you can't be here anymore
i'm sorry we never got the chance to grow old
to experience life together

i hope you know how much of an impact you've made on me and the
world
you changed me for the better
you made me realize how important it is to be kind and bring a little light
to those around me

i'm sorry you're not here, but i can feel you with me
i can feel you helping me to fight this
i will always do a little bit of what i do just for you
because you never got the chance to

happy birthday, anna
i love you forever

strength

strength is feeling weak
but doing the hard thing anyway

strength is facing something that feels impossible
but taking it on anyway

strength is letting the tears flow
and moving on regardless

strength is knowing you can do it
but not wanting to have to
and still doing it anyway

being strong isn't easy
and sometimes you are forced to be
but it is something to be acknowledged and to be proud of regardless

puzzle

just as i thought i was putting the pieces together
i have fallen apart

the pieces are scattered everywhere
but why? who did it?

it was me. i did it to myself.
sabotaged by my own brain

i can't stop it
and i can't help it
i just wish it would stop
so the puzzle of me could be put back together again

a little girl

inside i am still a little girl
even though i tried my best to bury her
even though i demeaned and tortured her over and over again

she's still there
and i'm sorry for her
because she didn't ask for this

she was taught to hate her body
she was taught that she was expected to succeed, to excel, to be
something great
she was taught that life is a grind, never failing to work for what you
want

she began to realize that she wasn't
pretty
wanted
enough

she tried everything in her power to live up to the expectations
formed in her mind
until she broke

she's been healing
but the cracks are still there
even when she forgets about them
sometimes they open back up
and swallow her whole

i'm sorry, child
i'm sorry you have to endure the pain
i'm sorry you were forced to be strong
i'm sorry you had to work so hard to be okay
i hope that one day you are
and i hope your heart shines through
just like it did when you were young

home

my home does not feel like a home
it is now filled with ghosts
old versions of me
it is a museum of a life past
filled with relics of my pain

i watch in my room as i relive mental breakdowns
i step over myself sprawled across the floor

i look in the same mirror,
and looking back is the very thing i was afraid to see
all those months ago
that mirror was the one i gazed in to look for a single ounce of adequacy
it's the same mirror in which i looked myself in the eye
searching for myself
and seeing a girl desperately grasping for a reason why

i lay in my bed and am thrown back to nights spent
scrolling through my camera roll, tearing myself to shreds
hopeless nights where all i could do was gaze at the ceiling
as my mind went rampant
nights where i cried myself to sleep,
ending one day and wondering if i could do another

i have grown and healed a lot since then
but those memories and emotions are sill raw
and that version of me isn't completely dead
there's still some broken parts of me
and being home just reminds me
like a would ripped back open
like a scar that never fully heals

scars

i watch as scars crawl up and down my body
part of me wants to stop, but more of me thinks
i don't deserve to

the pain is my escape
the cuts symbolize an internal battle
lost to myself
they symbolize pain deeper than any knife could cut
they are a manifestation of the turmoil inside me
because even though i've begun to heal in many ways
the broken parts still show

one day my scars will symbolize a battle won
because, like me, they will fully heal
with time and work and compassion and care

some may see scars and think i've damaged myself
when i see them, i will see strength
because i know the pain that caused them to be there
and i will know what it took for them to heal

triumph after loss
perseverance through temptation
light over darkness

eyes

they say they are the window to the soul
they show depths of emotion words cannot convey
and tell the authentic story that no amount of masking can hide

one glimpse and you can see
sadness
joy
emptiness
anxiety
hopelessness
pain

for months my eyes were dull and empty
then they were filled with pain
they would keep searching for a glimmer of hope
any sense of direction
a sliver of myself

on the hard days i look into my eyes to see how i'm actually doing
and i know
when i see the tired eyes
the empty eyes
that my soul is under attack once again

yet some days there is a little glimmer
a spark
hope
life

that wasn't there a few months ago
and i hope that my eyes continue to have that glimmer of life

a letter to my future lover

i doubt you will ever read this
but i've been waiting for you for a long time
i've always yearned to be wanted by someone
to be loved by someone
to be able to love someone
but there's a few challenges to loving me

sometimes i get sad, and i don't know why
sometimes i worry about small things
or i get stuck obsessing over the same thing over and over
sometimes i doubt everything and i need a lot of reassurance
i'm soft
i feel deeply
and i cry a lot
sometimes i shut down and you might think you've done something
wrong

i promise, darling, that it's not your fault
my brain just works a little different
it's really hard to understand sometimes
and even harder to explain

i have been through a lot
i've had to fight to be here
i now have scars on my body and painful memories in my mind
and i understand if i am too much to handle
i understand if i am too much to love

but i promise, dear, if you are able to love me
against all the odds
i will love you with everything in me
because one thing i know how to do is love

i will be caring and compassionate and understanding
i will do everything in my power to make you feel
content and valued and cared for
i will fiercely support you in whatever you do
i will be vulnerable in the hopes that you can have a space to be
vulnerable, too
i will be there for you no matter the circumstances
i will give myself to you
wholly and completely
because i care so much for you

and i hope that is enough
i hope that makes loving me worth it
i never thought it would be,
but maybe you will prove me wrong

my heart hopes you prove me wrong

friendship

it's a smile in the morning
silent waves goodnight
inside jokes only we can understand
a knowing look across the table

there are people that you get along with
and then there are people who get you
who you can be your unfiltered, authentic self around
without thinking twice
who are always there to listen
and not judge you
or lecture you
no, they will listen and they will care
and then they will give you a hug and assure you
that it will be alright

they will go out of their way
just to give you a moment of joy
and you know they will always be there for you

when you have a friendship like that, you don't take it for granted
you savor and protect it with your life
because they are the friendships that make
the days a little brighter
the nights a little shorter
the hard times a little more bearable

thank you for your friendship, my dear
i treasure it more than you'll ever know

pain is like a blanket

pain is like a blanket
not a warm and cozy one
no, it is itchy and scratchy and uncomfortable
it covers you until it's all you feel
it weighs you down

pain is like a blanket
once you're used to it, it provides a strange sort of comfort
you get so accustomed to always having it that it feels weird without it
feeling lighter feels like being exposed

pain is like a blanket
it keeps the feelings contained
it provides a shield to the rest of the world
it's my brain's way of keeping me under control

pain is like a blanket
i drag it around like i'm linus
and every time i think i've grown out of it, i return to it
i'm attached to it; it feels like a part of me
and i'm afraid that i'll never be able to let it go

i wonder

sometimes i wonder if the people i love know
just how much i care for them
how i would give every last piece of myself for them
how even just a few moments spent together means the world to me
how my heart leaps with joy when anyone thinks to invite me to anything

sometimes i wonder if i was just meant to be alone
that there will always be some parts of me that others never know
and that i will always have to resort to handling things myself

i do everything in my power to make people know
they're appreciated and wanted
and how much i enjoy being with them
because i never want anyone else to feel how i have
if i can do anything about it

chapter 6
feeling

mourning what wasn't mine

my body has changed
it's changed *a lot*
in fact, it's the biggest body i have ever lived in
and it is excruciating

i scroll through old pictures
romanticizing my smaller form
i gaze in the mirror and wish i could shrink myself back
it hurts *so much*

but more than anything
there is this deep, swelling sadness
because i know i can never have that body back
unless i sacrifice everything

i am not sure that i am capable of loving this body
or even being neutral about this body
not when i know what it once was
not when i only felt a sense of accomplishment, worth, and beauty
when it was smaller

but the fact is that i stole that body
i bartered with the devil to have it
to live in it for a short, precious while
but it wasn't mine to keep
it was dying
killing me slowly
and was hell to live in

the pictures don't show that, but i know the truth
and no deal could make it worth going back

remember

remember how you've given to get to this point
you had everything taken from you by your own mind
and you've fought to get it back and more

remember all of the times when no one was watching,
but you still showed up for breakfast?
remember the meals you dreaded showing up to, but did?
remember in program when you were scared out of your mind, and
your entire being was screaming at you,
but you won anyways?
remember every meal you finished while fighting through tears?
the times where you broke down over your body,
and still showed up for dinner?
the meals where you had to remind yourself to chew, where nothing felt
more impossible,
but you completed it anyway?

you pushed yourself our of your comfort zone
you began to honor your hunger when it felt wrong
you gave up exercising and are finally getting that back
"i gave my blood, sweat, and tears for this" applies wholly to you

and a number on a scale can't take that away
it isn't good enough of a reason to throw it away
trust that one day, it won't break you like it does now
trust that one day, it will truly be worth it

keep going, love
it will all be worth it in the end
and you are stronger than you know

tired pt. 2

i'm tired of pushing
i'm tired of having to put effort in to exist
i've made so much progress
progress that i've fought tooth and nail for
and yet i have so much further to go

every time i think i'm doing better
that maybe, *just maybe*, i'm putting dark days behind me
i am sucked back in
and those familiar feelings and thoughts return

i feel tired, the kind where i wake up wanting to go back to sleep
and my whole being feels heavy
no food seems appealing
i get hungry, but i'd rather feel the hunger than go through
the unpleasant process of eating
i somehow feel numb and want to bawl at the same time,
although i'm not sure why

and more than anything i feel alone
because i have no good reason to feel this way
and the few friends who i can go to are far away
and i don't want my family to worry
i don't want to be more of a weight on anyone than i already am
god, what i would give to cry into my friend's arms while she strokes my
hair and tells me it'll be okay
but instead i hold myself
try to keep my sobs silent
and dry my tears before i can be seen

i'm scared that i'll always go back to being this way
to feeling this way no matter how hard i try
and i'm scared that, at the end of the day,
i'll always be alone
that i just need to learn to deal with it myself
because at the end of the day
as unfortunate as it is
i am the only person who will always be there

loving

i was built to love
i need it like water
my heart explodes with it
i have so much to give

so i love recklessly
even when it hurts
even when it isn't reciprocated
i don't care

because who am i if i don't love others?
what is my purpose if it isn't to give?
what is life if you don't love?

i know i am loved by others
my family, siblings, friends
but i have never been able to show it to myself
and i have never received it romantically

i yearn for it
i want it so bad
because i think my mind needs someone else to prove that i can be
loved
that i *deserve* to be loved
before i can fathom giving an ounce of it to myself

christmas

a year ago, christmas felt hollow and empty
i had never felt more hopeless in my life
looking into the next year, i couldn't even bring myself to imagine the
next christmas
and in the following year there were moments where i questioned if i'd
make it there

but i did
i made it
and even though the past weeks i've felt empty and sad
and a bit broken
this morning i woke up feeling a little lighter
a little more at peace
a little more hopeful

maybe it's christmas magic
something i couldn't explain
but as i sat with my family and opened gifts and laughed and joked
my heart was filled with gratitude

gratitude that i did make it
that i could enjoy it
that i have so many loved ones
that i am so blessed

i'd lost hope that christmas could still be good
but i was wrong
it's still the beacon of joy and hope that i've always loved and cherished
and maybe the one i need the most

breaking

i feel like i'm breaking breaking breaking
tears stream down my face
there is a rift in my chest, in my soul
it clutches me tight, holding me captive

tomorrow will be three weeks sh free
and my mind is screaming at the thought:
you are disgusting
you don't deserve it
every scar on your body belongs there. and more.
much, much more.

there are scars already left behind
the scars that encapsulate my struggles
the scars that i deserve
as a reminder of what i've endured

there has always been a sliver of doubt
that i shouldn't escape this
that it would be a long, long while until it stopped
that probably, eventually, it would
just not anytime soon

it hasn't been bad or severe enough for it to end
i haven't done my time yet
i'm not yet qualified to say that i've struggled
to finally stop

when will it be enough?

i wish

i wish i could borrow my smaller body
just for a bit
so i don't stick out like a sore thumb

i wish i could be naturally small
that i didn't have to look like this
instead of what i used to

i wish i could fully fit in
to feel wanted
because even when i'm included
and even when i'm not alone
i feel lonely

i wish i had better skin
i wish i wasn't ugly
i wish i didn't have scars to hide
i wish i felt genuinely wanted

i could wish upon a million stars
flip a thousand pennies in a pool
but i will never be small
and i can't make myself fit in
i can't change any of these things
so i'm left with unanswered wishes streaming through my mind
day in and day out
and only a bit of disappointment and emptiness in my soul

feeling

i used to think that it was bad to express emotions
a sign of weakness and immaturity
successful people are strong
and they don't let emotion interrupt their work

i became an expert at hiding my feelings
there was not enough space in my life for them
not enough time to deal with them

but the truth is that i have big feelings
i love deeply, care deeply, feel pain deeply

i always thought i shouldn't care, but i do
and i hate that
or at least, i always have

but you know what?
i'd rather care too much than not at all
i'd rather love and get hurt than not love at all
i'd rather feel deeply than not at all
because that's what makes me human
and that's what makes me, me

i think i have a good heart
and i haven't hardened it despite anything i've been through
that's something to be proud of

so i'm glad i've learned how to feel again
i wouldn't have it any other way

alone in a crowded world

to the girls who walk alone behind the group
who only get sat next to on the bus when there's no other seats open
who have to scramble to be a part of any group project
who stand outside of groups of people
excluded from the conversation
who gather the courage to contribute something
just to be ignored
so they learn that what they say means nothing

to the girls who yearn to get an invitation
but then when they do they feel like it's only because of pity
that they aren't actually wanted
who wish they had that group, but find that they float between them
none ever seem to stick
so they begin to believe they are unwanted

to the girls who never get admiring glances
who never seem to get any attention in a crowd
who feel like every look at them is a look of
judgement or pity or both
so they learn they are flawed and unworthy

i see you
i am you
i hope you find your people
i hope you are accepted and appreciated for what you are
not excluded for what you are not
and i hope that someday you know, deep in your soul,
that you are worthy and wanted
and perfectly okay just as you are

the other girl

i've always wanted to be like that girl
the one who has clear skin
whose hair seems to fall just right
whose clothes seem to have been made for her body

i wanted to be like the girl who socializes with ease
floating about the world
catching the attention of anyone around her
she doesn't have to search for love or company
it comes to her

she seems so self-assured
she knows how to dress and do her makeup
the ins and outs of being female
she has her shit together

oh, i'm sure she has her problems
her own doubts and insecurities and struggles
but i'd rather have hers than mine

but what if, to others, i'm that girl?
the one who succeeds in school
does a million tasks in a day
who seems so put together

but i know the mess i am inside
how desperately i wish i was anyone but me

we all wish we could have what we don't
so i'm starting to think "that girl" doesn't exist
there are girls, all uniquely beautiful and different
and all flawed and hurt in ways that no one can see

kidnapped

i finally feel a bit better
like the worst days are behind me
that i might be able to live a little more

but then, out of nowhere, my mind returns to take me back
it throws shackles on me, chains me down
roughly grabs me
tries to drag me back to where i was before

i can't go
no. no. **no.**
i beg and plead and barter
my words become more panicked and desperate with each breath

no, please, no
i can't go back
i can't return to that darkness
that helplessness
that hopelessness
someone, please, hear me
save me
pleaseplease*please*
donttakemedontdoitimbegging
anything. i'll give you anything. just please leave me

i kick and scream and thrash and drag my feet
my entire being fights and protests
because now that i've had a taste of the light
i will give everything to keep it

chapter 7
growing

be here now

pause
take a breath
take a second to just *be*

it's easy to get overwhelmed
and stuck inside your head
to wish to escape
for this time to end

but you're here
living, breathing, heart beating
it feels impossibly hard but you're doing it
it's been difficult, but you're still here

this life, your life, is beautiful
it is fickle and sometimes unkind
but it is full of love and emotion
people and places and sights and sounds

and despite everything
what you've lost
the pain you've felt
the moments of darkness
you have this moment

you are here now, and that is what matters
as long as you are here, there is hope that it will all be okay
and if you pause for a moment
and look closely
you can see a bit of light
here
with you
right now

new perspective

i despise the changes in my body
it is bigger and softer than before
in all the wrong places
it has scars and stretch marks
it is weaker than it once was, long ago before it was destroyed and
broken down

but these things also symbolize everything i've endured
and how far i've come
i put myself through misery to gain this weight
these stretch marks are battle scars
left from fights i *won*
my body is soft because i finally softened my mind enough to listen to it
my scars are now *just scars*
the pain has left its mark, but now it's healing
just like me
i can't lift much or run very far
but that's because i had to give up my beloved exercise in order to heal
now this journey offers the opportunity to be stronger than i ever was
before
and to move for the joy of it, not as punishment

these things still feel like losses most days
but i'm starting to see a new perspective
one where these changes are okay
because they are due to a journey that has offered so much more

my old body could only hold a shell of me
my new one can hold all of me
and the person i am becoming

in this body
i laugh more
dance more
cry more
i sing at the top of my lungs
i feel deeper than i ever have
i have energy to do the things i am passionate about
i can finally *live*

i don't know if my body is still growing
but i know i still am
and i'm doing it in and because of this body
so from that perspective
it's not all bad after all

to be loved

i've never been in love
and no one has ever been in love with me

others write such beautiful words about it
i can only imagine what it's like
to have that fire burning within you
feelings of passion and desire and intimacy
feelings of security and safety
feelings of being truly wanted

to be looked at and touched like a treasure
to be given the world
and to give the world to another

i wish so badly to experience it
but i cannot fathom wanting me like that
i am beginning to think it is impossible
for me to be loved

growing

growing is hard
it takes a lot of effort and care
grace, rest, support
are the water, sunlight, nutrients
they're needed, but not always easy to give yourself or find
and it takes time to know exactly what you need to grow

growing takes time
it can be days, months, years and feel like you've gone nowhere
until you look at where you started and realized you have climbed an
entire wall
every bit closer to the sun than you were before

growing isn't neat or pretty
it takes twists and turns like ivy climbing a wall
sometimes you get stuck
have to crawl over jagged edges and across gaps
endure harsh seasons

but growth is still happening at every turn
you became stronger
and before you know it
you will be living in more light than you ever thought imaginable

independence

it's so easy to feel victimized by your mind
by whatever hard situations you've had to deal with
it's so easy to feel like you have no control
or like you are a little helpless

acknowledge it is hard
and know that it is not your fault

but know it is also possible to gain independence from this
to learn to live with it
to take back control
to make decisions that are good for you
despite your mind telling you not to
to care for yourself when you think you don't deserve it

you deserve to have this freedom
to be rid of the shackles that hold you back
that tarnish your life
it is independence that is worth fighting for

sitting with myself

the difference between being lonely
and being alone
is that loneliness is forced
but you can choose to be alone

i would never choose to be alone
because i could never sit with myself
i am my own greatest enemy
there could never be peace with just me

i've always hated that i was the only person that i always have
because i wished i could be free from myself,
not stuck with myself

but i am trying to learn
to sit with myself
to look in the mirror
and see a human being
not a monster
and instead of pulling out my sword for another battle
or putting up my shield to protect from another round of enemy fire
i want to reach my hand out
to find a companion
someone to rely on

because it's true
at the end of the day, i will always have myself
so if i want to have peace
i need to learn to sit with myself

stitches

healing feels like getting stitches
but with nothing to numb the pain
no painkillers, no sedative

poke, tug, repeat
each stitch hurts
you have no idea how long it will take for the wound to finally close
so you clench your jaw
dig your nails into the table
and persist until it is done

but when it is
you will be more free than ever before
but you will never forget the pain
a scar engraved on your soul

seeing the light

my journey is nowhere near over
i have grown and made progress in so many ways
but there are still many parts of me to heal

i used to think this path would have a distinct beginning and end
an old me and a new me
but i am now realizing that this is my life's work
ever growing
ever changing
becoming more myself and the person i want to be

i still have many dark days
days where i'm discouraged and want to quit
days where i feel lost and hopeless
but i have begun to see the light
recognize its presence amidst darkness
i now know this one truth:
the light always comes back

so i will continue to hold onto that
searching for it even when i doubt that it's there
because i know that whatever it takes to find it will be worth it
and it won't be for nothing
because the light *always* wins

acknowledgements

my journey, and this book, wouldn't have been possible without the love and support of so many people in my life.

my parents, who were there for me when i reached out for help and have been my rock the entire time.
my siblings, who have been a source of joy and light no matter how dark my mind was.
my friends, who were there through some of my hardest moments. you saw me break, get up, and break again. you sat with me through hard meals. you held me as i cried onto your shoulder, gave me a place to sleep when being on my own felt impossible. you repeatedly assured me that you loved me, appreciated me, wanted me here, *needed* me here. you helped me find moments to escape the hell of my mind.

you saved my life. i will never be able to find the words to thank you enough for that.

and lastly, to my support team, natalia and tricia. you have witnessed this entire journey, helped me sort through the mess of my mind, and heal my relationship with food and myself. you made sure i was never alone in this.

to tricia especially: thank you for providing a safe space where i could share my experiences and dig deeper into myself than ever before. you guided me through every setback and cheered me on through every win (and continue to do so). it is because of you this book exists. i was able to be vulnerable enough to share these entries with you, and we would joke about me putting it into a book. i didn't think it would ever happen back then, but now it's become reality. without you, i wouldn't know how to navigate the darkness. and because of you, i have found the light. thank you.